RAMADAN: THE MONTH OF SHUKR

First published in Malaysia by
Tertib Publishing
23-2, Jalan PJS 5/30
Petaling Jaya Commercial City (PJCC)
46150 Petaling Jaya, Selangor
Malaysia

Tel: +603-7772-3156 / +6017-399-7411
Email: info@tertib.press
Website: www.tertib.press

First Edition: April 2021

Cataloguing-in-Publication Data is available
from the National Library of Malaysia.

ISBN: 978-967-2420-96-5

Author: Sidra Hashmani
Illustrator: Wendy Hendra (Yujie Studios)
Editor: Najibah Nasruddin
Layout and Typesetting: Sofea K
Printed in Malaysia

Ramadan: The Month of Shukr

This Book Belongs To:

"As salamu'alaikum Ibrahim! Ramadan Mubarak!" Ruhi yelled as she ran excitedly towards her cousin, Ibrahim.

"Wa'alaikum salam Ruhi. Ramadan Mubarak to you too!" he responded, cycling towards her.

"Are you fasting today?" asked Ruhi.
"Of course!" said Ibrahim.
It was the first day of the
beautiful month of Ramadan.
They were both fasting
for the first time.

Ruhi's mom said Muslims are encouraged to give charity to the needy in Ramadan. "Shall we make *iftar* packages for them?" asked Mom. "I'd love that!" said Ruhi.

3

On the way to the *masjid*, her mom reminded Ruhi it was important to increase their charity in Ramadan because it was also the month of giving. "Ramadan is the month of fasting *and* giving?" Ruhi thought. That's amazing!

4

The next day, they packed so many *iftar* packages! "Well done Ruhi and Ibrahim! Would you like to play outside now?" asked Mom. "Yes, please!" they said.

Ruhi and Ibrahim were playing ball when
two kids came up to them. "Can we play
with you?" asked the girl. "My name is
Hafsa and this is my brother, Omar."

"Of course! We love playing with new friends," said Ibrahim. They ended up playing together all afternoon.
7

"All this playing has made me hungry!" Ibrahim told Ruhi and his two new friends. "What do you want to eat for iftar today?" he asked.
grrrowl!!!
8

Ruhi started naming all her favorite food that she knew were going to be waiting for her at home.

"Dates, fruit salad, chicken soup... Maybe I'll ask if we can have some cakes too!" she said with her mouthwatering.

9

"I am going to eat so much until I burst!" said Ibrahim. They both laughed.
HA HA HA

They looked at Hafsa and Omar
who were both sitting quietly.
"What are you going to eat for *iftar*?"
Ruhi asked.

"We're not sure... *Insha' Allah*,
whatever our mom makes!"

It was almost time to leave. Ruhi and Ibrahim said goodbye to their new friends. They were ready to go home and dig into their delicious *iftar*.

As they were walking away, Ruhi and Ibrahim heard Omar said to his sister, "I hope we will get *iftar* packages from the *masjid*."

Hafsa nodded happily, *"Insha' Allah!"*

13

Ruhi and Ibrahim were shocked!
Did this mean that their friends
normally didn't have
enough food?

14

Feeling sad about their friends,
they both told their parents
what they had overheard.

"Can we send some food to them, please?"
asked Ruhi and Ibrahim.
Everyone agreed.

"Insha' Allah, we will send them all our favorite treats!" Ibrahim said happily, thinking about everything he was going to send them.

16

They also agreed to make *iftar* packages for their neighbors, relatives, friends and anyone who needs help.

As they sat down to make *du'a* before *iftar*,
Ruhi and Ibrahim were excited to finally eat and
drink. Their parents even bought presents for
them to celebrate their first fasts.

Ruhi's dad said that fasting reminds them of those who don't have enough to eat. "We should help and make *du'a* for them," said Dad.

They were reminded that Ramadan
was also the month of being thankful.
"*Alhamdulillah* for everything
that Allah has given us," they said.

Ramadan Mubarak!
From Ruhi, Ibrahim, Hafsa & Omar!
21

Narrated Ibn 'Abbas:

"The Prophet (ﷺ) was the most generous of all people and he used to become more generous in Ramadan when Gabriel met him. Gabriel used to meet him every night during Ramadan to revise the Qur'an together. The Prophet (ﷺ) then became more generous than the fast wind."

Sahih al-Bukhari

About the Author

Sidra Hashmani is a mother, a traveller and a dreamer.

Growing up between Houston, Texas, USA and Karachi, Pakistan, her interest in books was inspired by her mother and encouraged by her family.

After college and as a new mother, she moved to Madinah, Saudi Arabia, where she studied Arabic, Qur'an and Islamic Studies. Her interest in writing Islamic children's books is fueled by her passion to make Islam at the center of her family life.

Sidra is currently residing in Houston, Texas, USA, with her husband and three children.

www.tertib.press

www.ingramcontent.com/pod-product-compliance
Lightning Source LLC
Chambersburg PA
CBHW080731120726
48001CB00010B/3199